FAVRE

MOST VALUABLE PLAYER

TEXT BY BRETT FAVRE   PHOTOGRAPHY BY MARC SEROTA

PHOTOGRAPHY & PICTURE EDITOR
MARC SEROTA

EDITOR
MARK VANCIL

DESIGNED & PRODUCED BY:
RARE AIR MEDIA
1711 NORTH PAULINA
CHICAGO, IL 60622

PUBLISHED BY:
EGI PRODUCTIONS INC.
224 THREE ISLAND BLVD., SUITE 102
HALLENDALE, FL 33009
954.455.1292
EGIINC@AOL.COM

DISTRIBUTED BY:
TRIUMPH BOOKS
601 SOUTH LASALLE STREET
CHICAGO, IL 60605
312.939.3330

SPECIAL THANKS

BONITA FAVRE AND THE FAVRE FAMILY

COOK & STEEN LAW OFFICES
BUS COOK
ONE WILLOW BEND DRIVE
HATTIESBURG, MS 39402
TEL: 601.264.9490
FAX: 601.264.5377

SPORTS MARKETING MANAGEMENT GROUP, LLC
11 E. KILBOURN, SUITE 2800
MILWAUKEE, WI 53202
404.277.6780

JOE SWEENEY
BRIAN LAMMI
DAN CARY
SONNY BANDO
MIKE HAYES
KATIE HOUSE
CHIP KELLEY

BRETT FAVRE'S STEAK HOUSE
MILWAUKEE, WI AND GREEN BAY, WI

SPECIAL THANKS TO LEE REMMEL AND THE ENTIRE GREEN
BAY PACKERS FOOTBALL ORGINIZATION

AT KODAK: TIM MCCABE, CANON EOS CAMERAS

AT TRIUMPH
MITCH ROGATZ, PETER BALIS, BILL SWANSON

AT RARE AIR MEDIA
MARK VANCIL, JIM FORNI, JOHN VIECELI, MARK ALPER,
SHEREEN BOURY, RICK DREWES, CHRISTY EGAN,
LIZ FULTON, MELINDA FRY, SETH GUGE, HEIDI KNACK
& LAURA YATES

AT THE NFL
PETE ABITANTE, DAN MARINO, JOHN ELWAY

AT EGI
SCOTT GOLDMAN/SALES & MARKETING
STEVE REICH/LEGAL COUNCIL
NESTOR NEYRA/MULTIMEDIA
ELISE KRIGE GLADING/INTERVIEWING

FOR INSPIRATION & SUPPORT
BOB & SANDY SEROTA, JOHN MAGGI, ROB DUYOS,
JEREMY & MICHELLE DYSCH & THE SANTANA FAMILY

JENNY SANTANA/CREATIVE DIRECTOR & UNCONDITIONAL
LOVE, HEART & SOUL.

TRIUMPH
BOOKS
601 South LaSalle Street
Chicago, Illinois 60605

EGI Books may be purchased for educa-
tional, business or sales promotional use.
Send inquires to Sales and Marketing,
EGI 224 Three Island Blvd., Suite 102,
Hallendale Florida 33009.

MVP
CHAPTER 1

CONTENTS

0:06

THIERRY
91

MVP
CHAPTER 2

MVP
CHAPTER 3

0:18

0:78

MVP1

0:07

IF YOU'RE PLAYING FOOTBALL

AND YOU LOVE THE GAME, THEN YOU ARE GOING TO DREAM ABOUT THE NATIONAL FOOTBALL LEAGUE.

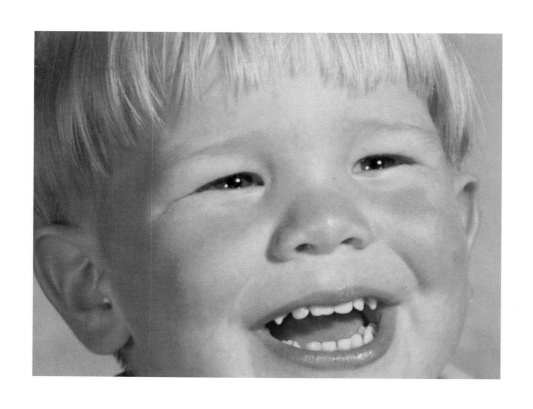

`0:08`

We didn't have very much growing up and my dad, Irvin, was the high school football coach. He was tough on us. I have two brothers and we all played quarterback for him. Nothing came easily and nothing was given to us, either. When I came out of high school, I wasn't recruited by anyone. I got offered the last scholarship at Southern Mississippi because a guy backed out. I wasn't anything like a lot of these high school quarterbacks who can pick whatever school suits them. I didn't have anybody coming after me. That's why I've never had a hard time appreciating the success I've had. It's a lot easier when you come up from the bottom and the bottom isn't that long ago.

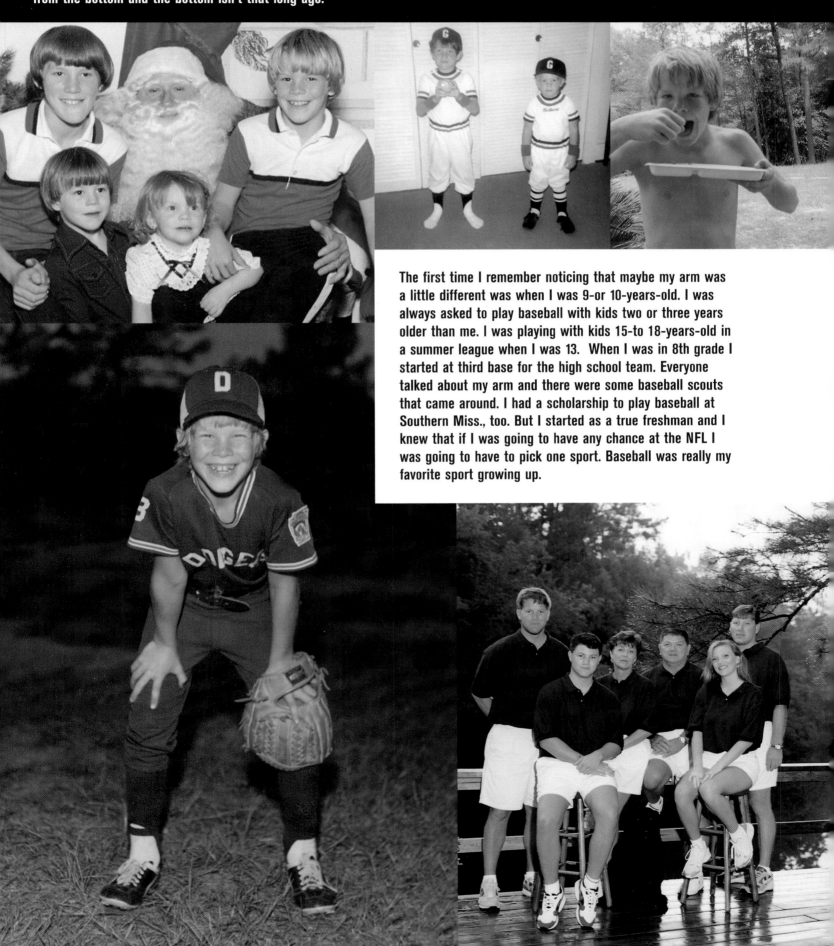

The first time I remember noticing that maybe my arm was a little different was when I was 9-or 10-years-old. I was always asked to play baseball with kids two or three years older than me. I was playing with kids 15-to 18-years-old in a summer league when I was 13. When I was in 8th grade I started at third base for the high school team. Everyone talked about my arm and there were some baseball scouts that came around. I had a scholarship to play baseball at Southern Miss., too. But I started as a true freshman and I knew that if I was going to have any chance at the NFL I was going to have to pick one sport. Baseball was really my favorite sport growing up.

I ALWAYS HAD WORN NO. 10 IN HIGH SCHOOL. THAT WAS MY FAVORITE NUMBER. WHEN I GOT TO SOUTHERN MISSISSIPPI, I ASKED FOR NO. 10 BUT THEY SAID THAT WAS REGGIE COLLIER'S OLD NUMBER AND THEY THOUGHT THEY MIGHT RETIRE IT. THE ONLY NUMBER THEY HAD LEFT WAS NO. 4. IN COLLEGE YOU HAVE 100 OR SO GUYS ON THE TEAM AND MOST OF THE OTHER NUMBERS WERE TAKEN BY THE RECEIVERS, RUNNING BACKS OR QUARTERBACKS, SO NO. 4 WAS THE ONLY ONE LEFT. IT DIDN'T SEEM LIKE THE RIGHT NUMBER AT THE TIME BUT IT SURE DOES NOW.

GROWING UP I HAD THE SAME DREAMS A LOT OF KIDS HAVE. I'D TAKE A FOOTBALL INTO THE BACKYARD WITH MY BROTHERS AND PRETEND I WAS THE QUARTERBACK IN THE SUPER BOWL.

0:12

IT WASN'T LIKE EVERYONE KNEW I'D BE A PROFESSIONAL FOOTBALL PLAYER.

I did play quarterback in high school at Hancock North Central High School, but our offense relied primarily on the run. I threw maybe 10 times a game as a senior. I knew I could throw the ball, but my father believed in driving the ball down the throat of the defense.

SOUTHERN MISSISSIPPI WAS THE PERFECT PLACE FOR ME TO PLAY AFTER HIGH SCHOOL.

I know a lot of NFL quarterbacks went to Florida State, Notre Dame, USC, UCLA and big schools like those but I wouldn't change a thing. If I had gone to one of those big schools I might not have played until my junior or senior year, if I played at all. The advice I give to young players is this: don't give too much credence to the aura of the school; go where you will play. Southern Mississippi obviously isn't Quarterback U. and it's not going to contend for a championship anytime soon. But look where I am today. I've accomplished a

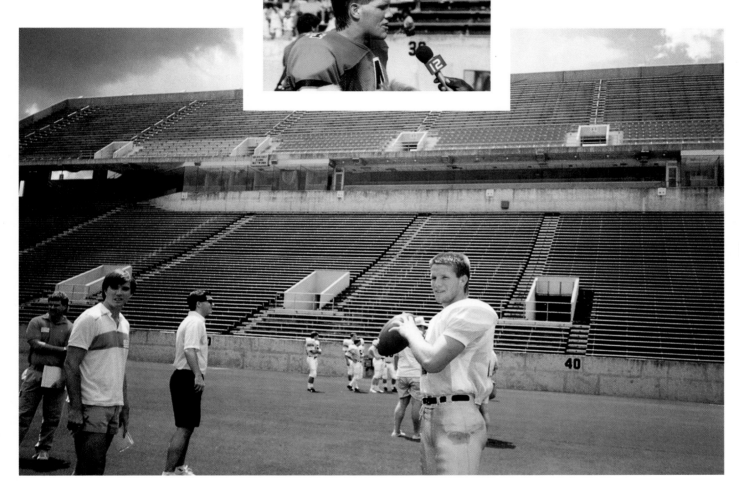

lot more than a lot of guys at those big schools ever will accomplish simply because I appreciated how hard it was to win ballgames and I was able to play every year. One of the things I attribute my early success to at Green Bay was the fact I played all four years at Southern Miss. Some guys only play one year of college football. They might have a great year, but they still don't know all of what is involved in a passing offense. They haven't seen enough. When I left college for the NFL I was 20-years-old. I had played four college seasons and I didn't redshirt. The 1999 season is my ninth NFL year and I'm still only 29-years-old.

I READ SOMEWHERE A LOCAL REPORTER SAW ME PLAY BASEBALL IN HIGH SCHOOL AND FIGURED I'D BE A MAJOR LEAGUE BASEBALL PLAYER IF I MADE IT AT ANYTHING.

I liked baseball, but I really loved to pitch. I always could throw hard, even though I never really worked on technique or anything like that. I just aimed and threw hard as I could, one pitch after another. One game, I think I struck out something like 15 guys, but I also hit a bunch. I hit three in a row at one point. I guess some of the hitters got pretty nervous up there, but I thought that was great. They moved off the plate a little more which turned out to be good for both of us. It just made me want to throw harder. I actually planned to play baseball my first year at Southern Mississippi. I thought all along I'd play both sports because I didn't expect to be playing much as a freshman. Remember, I was barely recruited out of high school. There wasn't a major college in the country that wanted me to play football for them much less become their quarterback. When I got to be the starting quarterback right away I decided I'd better get serious and learn all I could about football. It was the right decision, but sometimes I wonder what I could have done if I'd played baseball.

0:17

M V²P

0:19

IF I HAD STAYED IN ATLANTA AND NEVER CAME TO GREEN BAY, WHO KNOWS?

I might not even be playing. That first year with the Falcons I threw five passes and didn't complete one of them. I had no idea what was going to happen to me in Atlanta. I was a third-string quarterback and not really involved in anything going on there. The next thing I know I'm traded to Green Bay for a first-round draft pick. Everyone in Green Bay thought Ron Wolf, the general manager, was crazy. He got hate mail, fans were calling his office, house. They had no idea why Ron would take a chance on someone they never even had heard of before. It was a wake-up call for me. And it was a team that wanted me. When I look back, that's exactly what I needed.

I do think I was a little bit overwhelmed during my first few years in Green Bay. I went from being no one to BEING a household name almost over night. In a way, it wasn't a whole lot different than going from Hancock North Central High School to Southern Mississippi University. It seemed like I went from an afterthought to third string quarterback to starter in no time at Southern miss. The same kind of thing happened once I got to Green Bay. I was playing behind Don Majkowski. Don had a great year in 1991 and everyone knew he was the starter. But in 1992, in the third game of my first season in Green Bay, Don got injured in the first half against Cincinnati. I came in and we won the game 24-23 on a fourth-quarter touchdown pass to Kittrick Taylor with 19 seconds left. I started the next week against Pittsburgh and I haven't missed a start since.

0:21

MIKE HOLMGREN
AND I WERE OPPOSITES IN MANY WAYS.

Mike and I had different ways of doing things, but fortunately for both of us we met in the middle. It really worked–for us, for our team, for Green Bay–because we won rapidly. I did play my way, but I also listened to him and added his expertise to my game. It made me a different player. I was able to execute his offense the way he wanted but also throw in my 2 cents to make a difference. That's what won the MVP awards. I had big numbers, but I also looked for ways to make big plays that other guys couldn't make. Without that offense and without his leadership, I couldn't have done those things. So in that sense, it was a match made in heaven. We clashed from time to time, but it was beneficial. And the objective was totally the same.

0:23

THINGS WILL BE DIFFERENT WITH MIKE HOLMGREN NO LONGER THE HEAD COACH.
RAY RHODES IS A DEFENSIVE GUY
AND HIS COACHING STYLE IS A LOT DIFFERENT.

The offense won't change because Sherman Lewis is still the offensive coordinator. So the terminology and play-calling will be almost the same. Ray is a former player. Mike played in college, but he didn't play pro ball. Ray knows the locker room aspect of professional football. He comes down to the locker room and talks to guys. Mike's approach was a little different. His was more of a professional approach, more like an accounting job. Mike would tell you what you had to do and that was it. Ray is more likely to tell you to bust your ass and get your job done the best way you know how. Mike was real precise. He was a perfectionist. Obviously, it worked. That's not to say Ray isn't those things, but sometimes in Mike's approach you forgot some of the other things like knocking a guy in the mouth. So there are pros and cons to each side of it.

0:24

I might be totally wrong, but that's how comfortable I feel in this offense. I know I can think how Mike thought. It might not be as deep as he thought, but I know the plays and I know the plays he would call. So I felt comfortable with him leaving when he did. I'm sure I wouldn't have been as comfortable if he had left earlier in my career. I think it was the right time.

FEEL LIKE I COULD CALL THE PLAYS MYSELF.

0:27

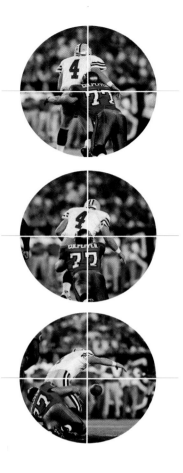

I KNOW FOOTBALL IS A
TOUGH GAME.

MY BODY KNOWS IT'S A TOUGH GAME.

I understand what you have to do to survive out there with all the pain, blood and back and forth between players. But I can't stand guys going for my feet, or throwing an illegal hit designed to knock me out of the game. The game is rough enough when it's played the right way.

If I get hit hard, I will try to get back up as quickly as possible. Sometimes it's instinct, other times I'm trying to get up to prove a point. Some times, what looks like a particularly hard hit really doesn't hurt at all. I think by getting up quickly it has to do something to the defense. It has to be thinking, `What do I have to do to hurt this guy?' Maybe that bouncing up and acting like you're not hurt even if you are gives me a little advantage. And I'll take any advantage I can get no matter how little. It may hurt and it may hurt badly on Monday morning, but if it helps us get an edge and win a ballgame that's fine.

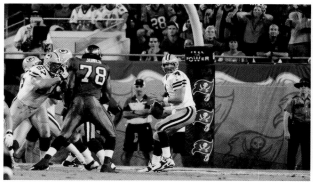

I don't consider the way I play the game as being out of the ordinary. I've been called tough, but I just think that's the way you should play. I don't know any other way to put it. There's only one way to play no matter what you're doing. I want to win and I will do whatever it takes to do that. If it means getting hurt and having my body get beat up, then that's part of it. I realize this job is tough on your body and it's tough mentally. It's not an every-day job where you walk into the office and a tough day is not meeting your quota. A tough day for me might be a broken leg. That's just part of my job. When I step onto the field I realize it could be my last time so I play it that way.

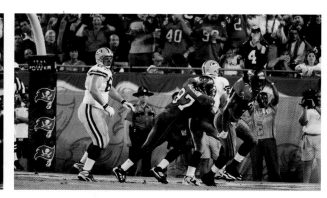

122 CONSECUTIVE GAMES

At 50 or 60 games the consecutive-game streak really `0:31` wasn't that big a deal. No one talked about it and I didn't realize I had started that many in a row. But now with a 122 straight going into the 1999 season, I have started to focus on it a bit because it just doesn't seem to happen these days. Whenever it ends, it's still a streak that will have been pretty unbelievable given today's game. Every year, four or five guys go down in the first couple weeks of the season. To think how reckless I play the game and that I've been able to withstand all the hits and injuries and still play well is something to be proud of. I think the hard work I've put into the game during the season and during the off-season has made a difference.

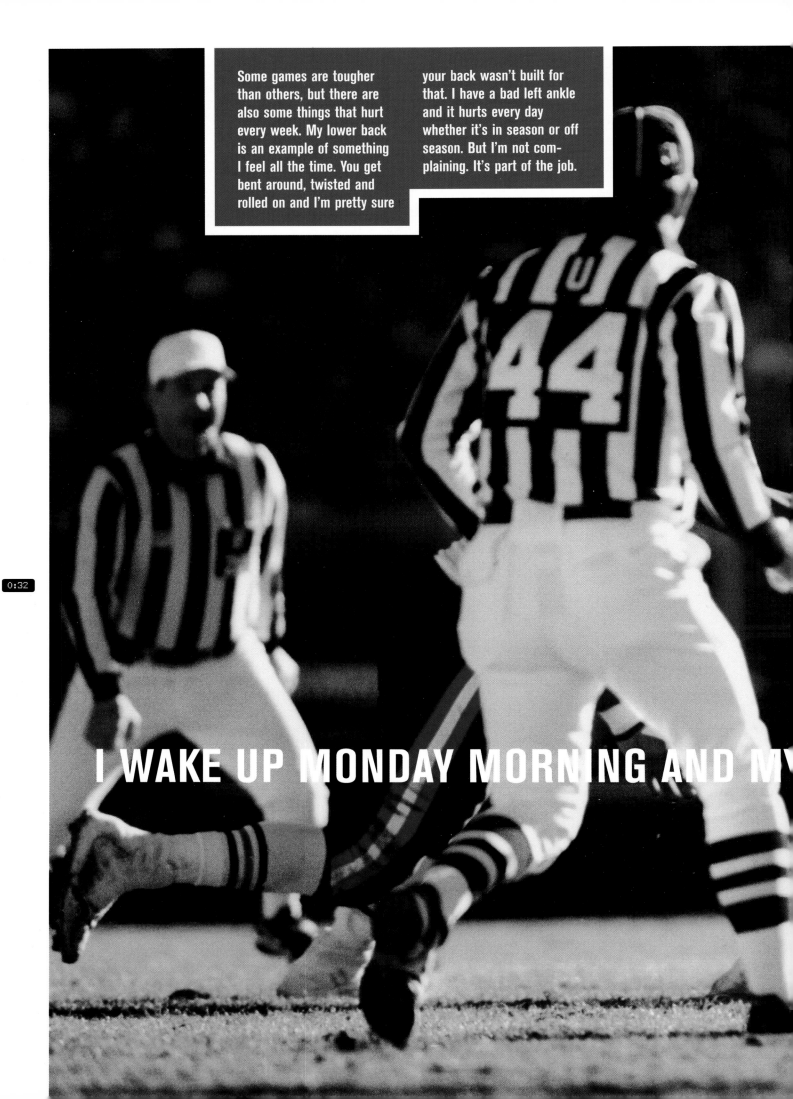

Some games are tougher than others, but there are also some things that hurt every week. My lower back is an example of something I feel all the time. You get bent around, twisted and rolled on and I'm pretty sure your back wasn't built for that. I have a bad left ankle and it hurts every day whether it's in season or off season. But I'm not complaining. It's part of the job.

I WAKE UP MONDAY MORNING AND MY

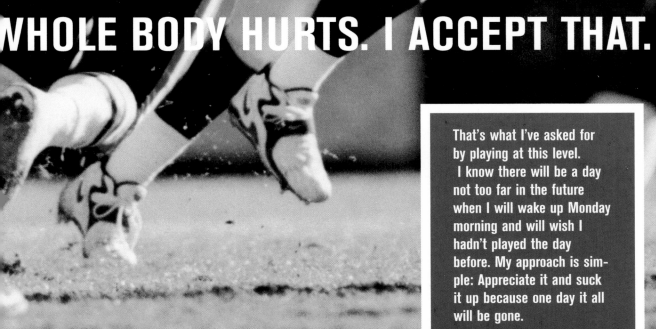

0:33

WHOLE BODY HURTS. I ACCEPT THAT.

That's what I've asked for by playing at this level. I know there will be a day not too far in the future when I will wake up Monday morning and will wish I hadn't played the day before. My approach is simple: Appreciate it and suck it up because one day it all will be gone.

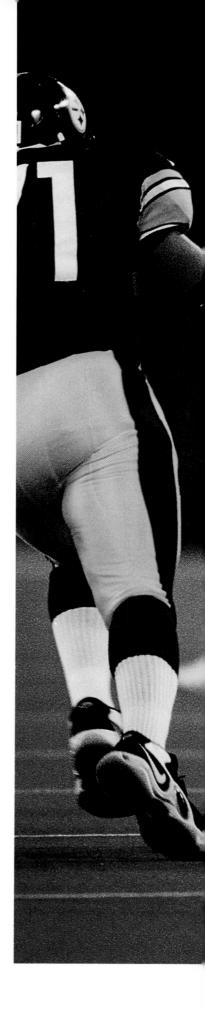

AT THIS POINT IN MY CAREER I KNOW I'M NOT
BULLETPROOF.

I know what can happen to your body out there. But I do think I'm pretty tough. I love the game, including the physical part. Sure, you take a beating. With all the hits that a quarterback gets, you need a little luck to go out and perform every week, every year. So you hope for some luck. But after that, all you can do is play hard and hope for the best. The whole show is only going to last so long. If I'm able, I want to be on stage every minute.

0:35

`0:36` Early in my career, I relied on my natural size and strength. At 29, I still can throw the ball as well as most guys in the league. But I never worked on it. I never warmed up and I never iced after throwing. I'd just go out and start throwing 50-yard bullets. As I got a little older I thought maybe I'd like to play six or seven more years. So I started working out a little bit and icing my arm after practice. I thought it might help me a little. Then, with each one of the MVP years, the next year I worked out a little harder. I always have been self motivated and now it's even greater. Once you realize the pains stay a little longer and time is passing by, you do what you have to to improve. I still want to be the best. There are days I wake up and work out hard. Then, just as I'm finishing I think maybe I'll do just a little more.

I want to be the best player I can be. There are some guys who experience some success and that's enough for them. They still play hard, but they are satisfied. I know I'll never be satisfied. I try to do everything I can to make me better. If I do that, then I know I can help our football team win games. That's why I put so much time and effort into my preparation off the field. If I'm not studying the play book or game plan, then I'm in the weight room. I want to be on the field every Sunday. I want to give myself and my team every opportunity to win no matter the situation.

People talk about leadership, but it's just like playing the game tough. In my opinion, there's only one way to lead and only one way to play the game. I don't like taking orders from anyone and I really don't like giving them either. But I do like doing things my way and I think my way is the best way. I've clashed with every coach I've ever had. I listen and I get along with them, but I even can remember arguing with my dad. That really hasn't changed. I've been told by every coach, every week, to slide when I'm about to get hit or to get out of bounds and avoid the hit. But that's hard for me to do. I want to get the first down or score the touchdown. They come back and say, 'Fine, but we want you around for the next play.' I say, 'Well, who knows? The play where you wanted me to slide might have been the play that won the ballgame for us.' That's the way I look at it. They're right and I'm right.

I FIGURE IF I'M IN THE WEIGHT ROOM AT 6 IN THE MORNING AND
DIVING FOR LOOSE BALLS
AND FIGHTING FOR FIRST DOWNS OUT ON THE FIELD,
THEN MY TEAMMATES SHOULD DO IT, TOO.

That's the only way to lead as far as I'm concerned. Going around and yelling at a guy who drops the ball isn't leadership. There are days I throw incomplete passes and interceptions and I don't want anyone chewing me out. You pat a guy on the butt and tell him to do better next time. Everyone has an opinion of a leader. To me, it's the guy who has everyone else wanting to do what he does.

I realized in 1995, when I was named Most Valuable Player, just how far I had come. I took a look at the list of previous winners and they all made sense. Guys like Steve Young, Joe Montana, Emmitt Smith, they all went to big schools. I'm sure those guys dominated at the high school level. Then they all were big stars at big colleges. That's why winning big awards such as the MVP always has been a little more special. No one would have expected me to be a starting quarterback in the National Football League much less be the Most Valuable Player. In high school, I was no different than the quarterback at St. Stanislaus or Pearl River Central. I was third string on the high school all-star team. Looking back though, I'm glad it worked out that way. The process was a lot longer and probably a little tougher, but I think that has helped me become the player I am.

MONTANA SMITH YOUNG

0:40

I still like those old guys, the quarterbacks that just beat you. They didn't look particularly good doing the job, but they always got it done. Everybody knows I like Billy Kilmer, Sonny Jurgensen, Bobby Layne, the kind of guys that had a reputation off and on the field. Look at Kilmer. He had a little pot belly in the middle of this little body. His shirt's hanging out.

ILMER LAYNE JURGENSEN

If he didn't have a uniform on, you would think he was a janitor or a truck driver. His nose is smashed up. He had blood all down his jersey, his arms, his sweatbands. Then he scrambles around on a 20-yard play, dives into the end zone and scores. I got chill bumps. How did he do it? He couldn't outrun anybody. He's slower than me and that's slow. But he found a way. That's what separates the great ones from the average ones. There are plenty of quarterbacks who can outrun me, probably out throw me and throw more accurately. But why aren't you hearing about them? What separates me from some other guy who's the same size as me, same speed, same arm and everything? It's the fire inside, the emotion. I love to play the game. Don't get me wrong, I like picking up the paychecks. But I can't wait for Sunday.

WHEN I LOOK AT FILMS OF OTHER QUARTERBACKS, IT SEEMS LIKE THE
GUYS WHO THROW HARD REALLY TAKE A BIG WINDUP AND I DON'T DO

LIKE I JUST PULL IT BACK A

0:42

THAT. TO ME, IT SEEMS LIKE I THROW LIKE A CATCHER IN BASEBALL. I SEE
MYSELF ON FILM AND THE BALL NEVER GETS BACK MUCH PAST MY EAR.

ITTLE WAYS AND THROW.

TO TELL THE TRUTH, I DON'T KNOW HOW I CAN THROW IT SO HARD.
I'M JUST GLAD I CAN.

0:43

I NEVER HAVE ADJUSTED TO THE WEATHER IN GREEN BAY.

0:44

0:45

I DON'T LIKE IT AND I DON'T THINK ANYONE CAN ADJUST TO THAT KIND OF COLD. THERE IS NOTHING FUN ABOUT 0 DEGREE WEATHER OR A FOOT OF SNOW.

didn't grow up in cold weather and I don't see any need to go out to ski or snowmobile. I don't do anything like that. I don't even go outside if I can help it. Usually, by the time the season is over, I have cabin fever. I'm ready to get home. I come home in January and February and I can go outside and play golf. I miss home, for a lot of reasons including weather. I don't think anyone likes playing in the kind of conditions we can have in Green Bay, but I have been successful playing that way. I think it's simple: I don't like it but neither does the other team. I know I have to play. What am I going to do? Quit and walk off the field on the days that are cold? I look at our schedule and realize we're going to have a few games late in the season that are going to be cold. We play Arizona late in the 1999 season. When the Cardinals get off the plane they are going to know something's not quite the same for them. But when I get up that morning and drive over the stadium I will have known for six months it was going to be cold that day. So I think there is an advantage to living in that cold and accepting the fact it's going to be that way.

I've been fortunate. I've stayed healthy for a lot of reasons. I think the offense enables me to do a lot of things, get rid of the ball quicker. It's not a deep-pocket offense. You don't stand back there and take a lot of hits. Now, the way I play the game I do take a lot of hits but I like to play that way. That's football to me. I keep myself in good shape so when I do get hit, sure I'll be sore the next day, but physically I'm able to withstand the punishment. Also, I think the way I throw the ball has something to do with my ability to avoid serious injury. I throw the ball differently than most guys. My feet are always moving. You'll never see me plant more than once or twice a game. My feet are almost always off the ground so when guys hit me I'm able to just fall and not get rolled up.

0:48

THERE'S NO ONE THING I LIKE OVER ANOTHER IN A RECEIVER.

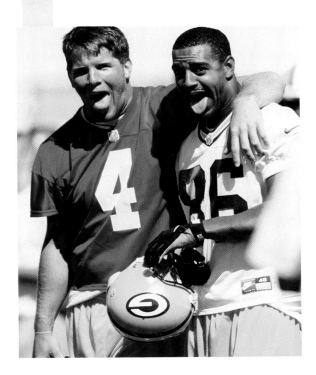

I've had guys who are fast, guys who are tall, some with better hands. To me, a complete receiver is a guy who can do it all. They don't have to be great at any one thing. Robert Brooks and Antonio Freeman aren't slow, but they aren't going to outrun most guys. They aren't as tall as some other guys and they can't outjump a lot of guys. What they do is work hard. They make big plays. They find a way to make plays when no one expects them to. They're tough and they work hard. That's all I ask for. Sterling Sharpe was that type of guy. He wasn't going to outrun anybody, but I could trust him in crucial situations. I feel that way about all our receivers.

People ask me about that sixth sense that kicks in and makes me get rid of the ball at exactly the right moment before I get hit.

You have to remember, there are only 30 of us starting every Sunday in the NFL. Of all the people in the world, only 30 have all

the tools necessary to compete for a professional football team every week. It's sort of like a neurosurgeon or rocket scientist.

There are only a few people who even want to attempt to have a career like that. Then there are even fewer who actually can do

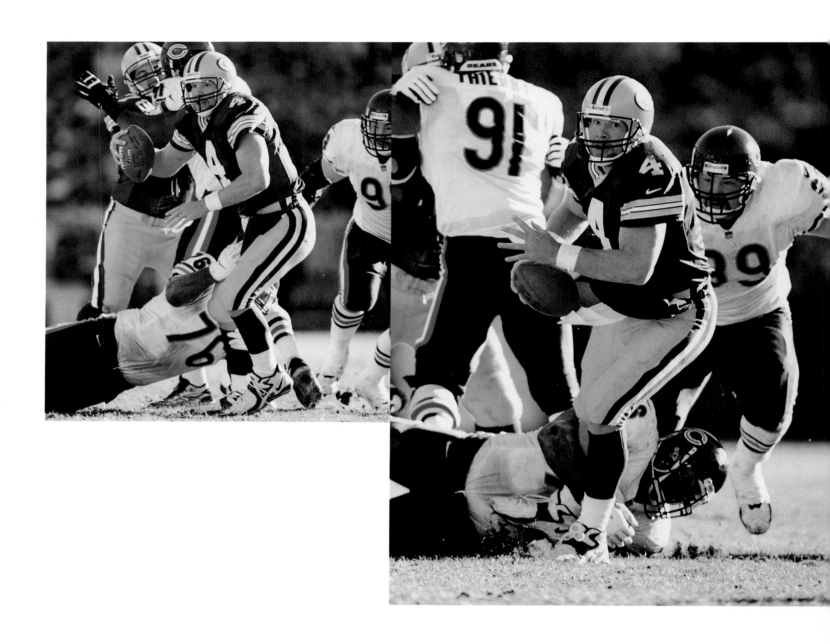

it. Growing up I thought I wanted to be an electrical engineer. I realized I couldn't do it . There are lot of guys out there who want to be quarterbacks, too, and trying harder probably isn't the issue. The reality is I couldn't be an electrical engineer. No matter how much I tried, that's not something I could do. There are probably a lot of people born to be a pro quarterback who still don't make it. There is something that separates us from all those other quarterbacks. Just like the neurosurgeon has something that separates him from other doctors. I can't do what he can do, but I doubt he could feel the rush coming from his blind side. I don't have the steady hand to operate on a brain, but I can feel the rush and still complete a 30-yard comeback, get bopped and bounce back up and throw a touchdown, all while 60,000 people are screaming. There are different things the separate all of us in our line of work some of them are greater than others. The thing about football is that while I'm doing my job somebody's trying to knock me on my rear. Most people wouldn't consider that normal. Then again, if that neurosurgeon had 60,000 people watching him and yelling every time he made a move, that would add a degree of difficulty.

Reggie White was the one defensive line-man concerned me the most before he joined the Packers. I played against him when Reggie was at Philadelphia my first and second years in the league. As just about every quarterback eventually realized,

PLAYING AGAINST REGGIE

But as a teammate, they don't make 'em any better than Reggie White. I remember one Sunday during the 1998 season. We were sitting on the bench and Reggie looked over at me. He said, "I love you." And I looked back at him and said, "I love you, too." And we meant it. I really hoped he would play another year. I know I won't be the only one that will miss having him around.

Some players don't like the media because of what is said or written about them. I don't worry about it. I do have some control over what is written and what others say about me or my performance. If I go out there and play an average game and the press writes about it, why should I be angry? If I play a great game, everyone will pick up the paper and read all the wonderful things about me. I see both sides. The only thing I ask is that the press doesn't make anything more than what it is. In other words, don't exaggerate. If I play a good game, just write that I was good. Don't say, "He is the greatest quarterback in the history of the game." Same thing goes when I play poorly.

0:54

My philosophy concerning members of the press is simple:
THEY ARE DOING THEIR JOBS.

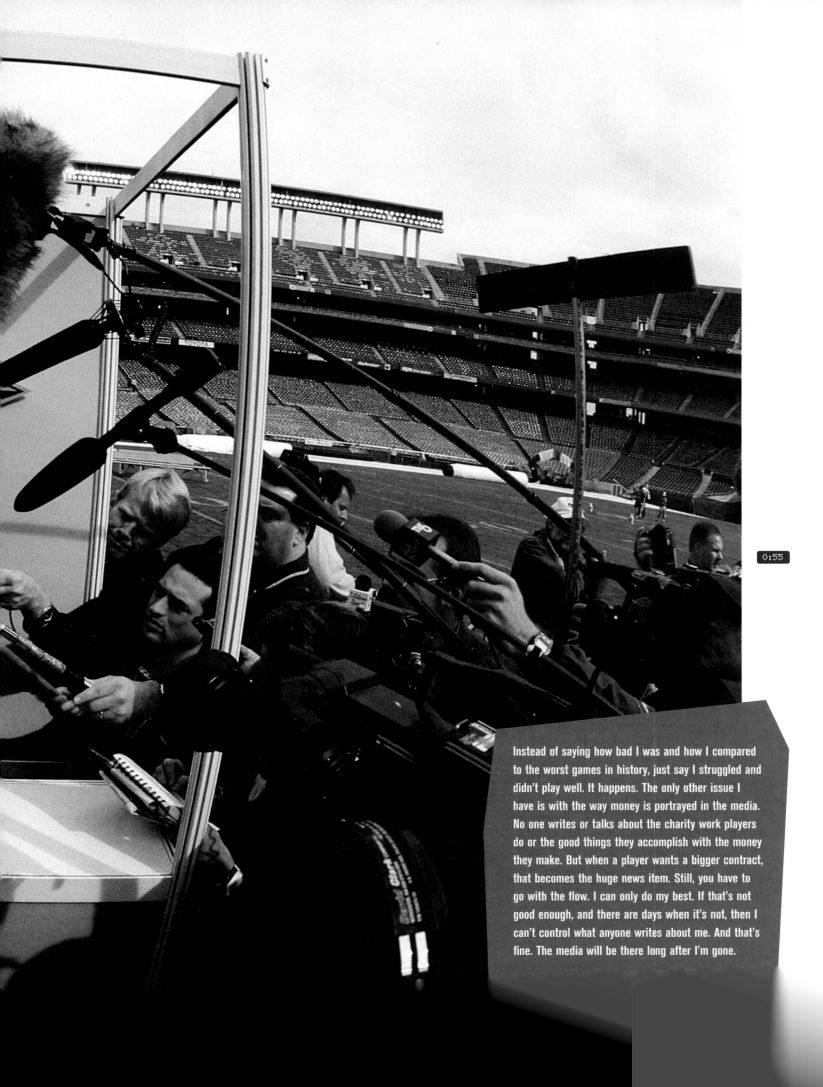

0:55

Instead of saying how bad I was and how I compared to the worst games in history, just say I struggled and didn't play well. It happens. The only other issue I have is with the way money is portrayed in the media. No one writes or talks about the charity work players do or the good things they accomplish with the money they make. But when a player wants a bigger contract, that becomes the huge news item. Still, you have to go with the flow. I can only do my best. If that's not good enough, and there are days when it's not, then I can't control what anyone writes about me. And that's fine. The media will be there long after I'm gone.

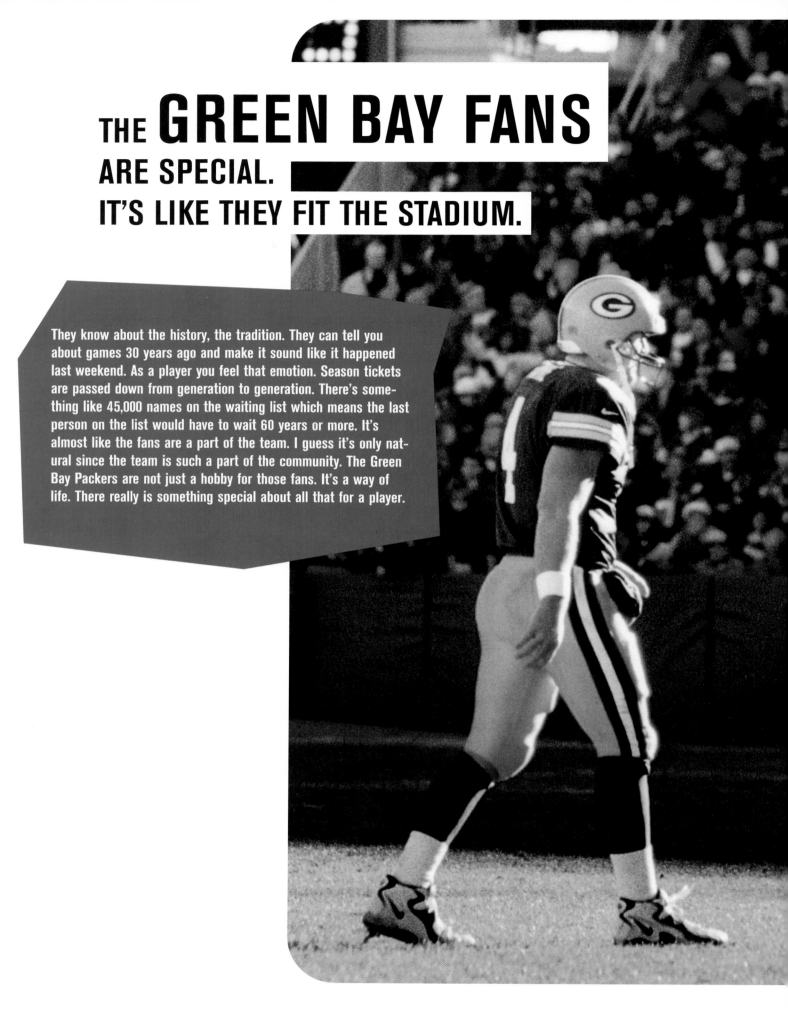

THE GREEN BAY FANS ARE SPECIAL. IT'S LIKE THEY FIT THE STADIUM.

They know about the history, the tradition. They can tell you about games 30 years ago and make it sound like it happened last weekend. As a player you feel that emotion. Season tickets are passed down from generation to generation. There's something like 45,000 names on the waiting list which means the last person on the list would have to wait 60 years or more. It's almost like the fans are a part of the team. I guess it's only natural since the team is such a part of the community. The Green Bay Packers are not just a hobby for those fans. It's a way of life. There really is something special about all that for a player.

THERE IS SO MUCH HISTORY IN LAMBEAU

and to think I am a small part of that history is an honor. You can't help thinking about all the great players who have played there and what they have done for the franchise. There's something special about walking out onto that field. It's like you can feel the history, the tradition.

THERE IS NOTHING PREMEDITATED ABOUT MY EMOTION ON THE FIELD.

0:60

NOT ME.

I'm truly caught up in the moment. That's why the game is so fun for me. Every touchdown is like the first one. No matter how many I throw or how many we score as a team, that never will change. I never have scored a touchdown when I felt, well, it's just another day at the office. I always have believed my ability comes through because I play the game from the inside out. The passion you see is real. The day I don't feel a

SOME PLAYERS THINK ABOUT HOW THEY LOOK

WHEN THEY CELEBRATE A BIG PLAY.

rush of adrenaline after a touchdown is the day I'll know I have to walk away. I have respect for the game. I know it's a game, but I also know how the game should be played. When you step on the field, that should be your sole focus. When you are totally into that moment, the ups and downs are amazing. It's the emotion that comes from being comfortable with letting it all hang out. That way you never know what to expect, which makes an exciting job even more rewarding.

I don't know if I would have liked playing an individual sport like tennis or golf. I like the idea of being a part of a team. It always has been important to me. You see athletes who try to single themselves out as individuals, but to be successful, especially in this sport, you have to be part of a team. Teams win Super Bowls, not individuals. Every player has to buy into that idea because all of us rely on each other. You have to be able to trust the guy next to you. For me to do my job I need linemen to block for me, receivers to catch the ball and coaches to call the right play.

0:62

THE TEAMS THAT PLAY TOGETHER
THE BEST ARE THE TEAMS THAT WIN.
IT'S THAT SIMPLE. TALENT COMES INTO PLAY, BUT
TALENT ALONE CAN'T WIN FOOTBALL GAMES AT THIS LEVEL.

FOOTBALL IS A

even more than most fans can appreciate. I play golf with a lot of former players such as Paul Hornug and Tom Jackson. Tom played in my golf tournament over the

summer and for the first time I noticed how much trouble he had just getting out of a golf cart and walking up to the golf ball. And he's not that old. He struggled. Mike Ditka has had two hip replacements. Paul Hornug was one of the greatest running backs in the history of the game but if you look at him now you would never know he played. You take a perfectly gifted athlete, which virtually everyone is in the NFL, put him in this sport and 10 or 15 years later he looks like he has had some kind of disease all his life. Does it scare me? A little bit. I'm trying to do everything possible to stay healthy, but the reality is the game is getting more violent, the guys are getting bigger, faster and stronger. The days of a guy such as Dick Butkus being a 235-or 240-pound linebacker, even as mean as he was, and he

BRUTAL GAME,

was mean, are over. Now you have guys such as Reggie White who weigh 310 pounds and run 4.8-second 40-yard dashes. When they hit you full speed it's like getting hit by a car going about 5 m.p.h. over and over. No one recovers that quickly. Seven days is not enough, but that's what we have to do. As soon as you start getting over the previous week you go out there and do it all over again. It's different for every-one. Running backs get hit on every play. Quarterbacks don't get hit as often, but when they do they're usually just standing there taking the full force of the blow. We are paid the big bucks, so to speak, to drop back there to take the hits. So it's pretty tough on your body. But once again, it's part of the job. I do everything I can to

make myself strong enough to withstand the punishment so that I can move around when I'm older. I'm sure there will be a day when it will be time to get out. I remember John Elway in his retirement speech. He said he could keep playing mentally, but his body just wouldn't respond like it used to any longer.

I KNOW EVERYONE LOOKS AT

THE THREE MVP SEASONS,

BUT I KIND OF FEEL LIKE 1998
WAS AS GOOD A SEASON AS I'VE HAD.

We weren't as good because we had a lot of injuries. I did have eight more interceptions than the year before, but I still led the league in yardage and completion percentage and threw 31 touchdowns. Everyone said I had a down year, but we started four different tailbacks and went through a lot of changes. I felt like I was able to maintain the level of play I've had for the last four or five years. That's not easy to do in this league.

0:67

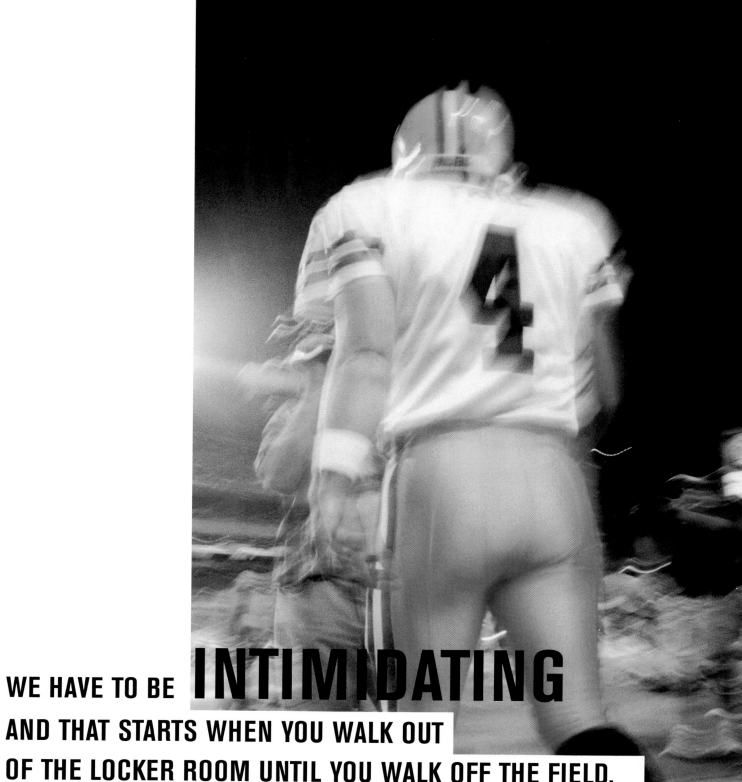

WE HAVE TO BE **INTIMIDATING** AND THAT STARTS WHEN YOU WALK OUT OF THE LOCKER ROOM UNTIL YOU WALK OFF THE FIELD.

When I was at Southern Mississippi and we played Auburn and Alabama and Florida State, I was scared when I walked out of the locker room door. My linemen were 220 pounds and their defensive linemen were 320. So obviously, there was the intimidation factor. When you walk out there, the other team has to look at you and know you are ready.

I ALWAYS HAVE THOUGHT I LEARNED MORE FROM

THE DEFEATS THAN THE VICTORIES.

We all want positive and nice things to happen to us, but somehow we learn more from the negative experiences. It's the same thing on the football field. It's how you react to bad situations that really shapes you. they let everyone else know who you are. That's why I try to maintain a positive attitude. No matter what happens, I want everyone around me to know we still have a chance. It's important my teammates know I might get knocked down, but I'm getting right back up.

Winning the Super Bowl in 1997 was the absolute highlight of my career. I remember walking out onto the turf in the Super Dome and looking around. Despite all that was about to happen I actually was thinking

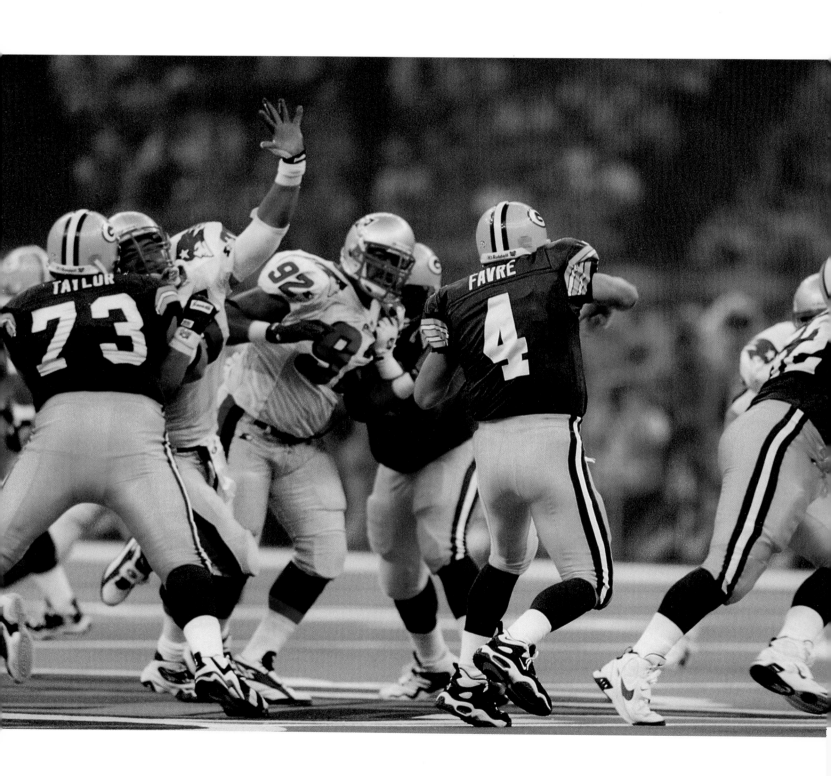

about the fact I was about to play a football game for a team in the Super Bowl. It's one of those dreams that you remember from childhood. There I was about to live out the same dream millions of kids have had.

`0:74`

I THINK BOTH **SUPER BOWLS**
MADE ABOUT THE SAME IMPACT ON ME PERSONALLY,

When we walked off the field inside the Super Dome I remember thinking, 'This has to be the greatest feeling I've ever had.' Then the next year was like the worst feeling I've ever had. It was like losing a loved one. The first one was like my daughter Brittany being born. And it came and went so quickly. You only have so many days and months to enjoy something great.

After about a week of wearing the Super Bowl ring I took it off and I've never worn it since. I knew that moment had passed and it was time to focus on the next challenge. I wasn't about to live in the past because I knew the next year would be tough.

BUT IT WAS ONE EXTREME TO THE NEXT.

Someday there will be another quarterback in Green Bay and if he's fortunate enough to play as well as I have and lucky enough to have had the success I've had, I hope he will see it all for what it is. One day it will be over. I know that. The people asking me for autographs will be asking the next guy.

SOME KID WILL SAY,

"WHO IS BRETT

just like they do Bart Starr. Bart Starr was at my golf tournament and the older people wanted to talk to him and get his autograph. The younger people had heard of him, but they didn't remember him. That will happen to me. But when that happens I'll have my same friends and I'll still be driving a pick-up truck. I won't have to worry about walking into a restaurant and having people look at me and think, 'Now he wants to be like us. Where was he 10 years ago?' I won't let that happen.

FAVRE?"

M
V
3
P

0:79

AS MUCH AS I LOVE FOOTBALL, AND I DO LOVE THE GAME, MY FAMILY ALWAYS HAS PROVIDED A FOUNDATION FOR ME. WITHOUT THEM, I KNOW I WOULDN'T BE WHERE I AM TODAY.

YOU DON'T REALIZE HOW MUCH SUPPORT AND ASSISTANCE THEY PROVIDE UNTIL YOU REALLY NEED THEM. THEN YOU

REALIZE THEY HAVE BEEN THERE ALL ALONG.

MY WIFE, DEANNA, AND I WERE TOGETHER FOR YEARS BEFORE WE MARRIED. SHE MOVED UP TO GREEN BAY AND I WON THREE MOST VALUABLE PLAYER AWARDS.

I STILL HAD TO GO OUT ONTO THE FIELD AND PERFORM, BUT I DON'T THINK IT'S A COINCIDENCE THAT MY GREATEST SUCCESS

HAS COME SINCE WE'VE BEEN MARRIED.

WE ARE BLESSED
WITH A WONDERFUL DAUGHTER.

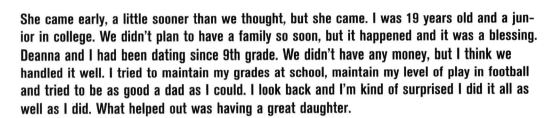

She came early, a little sooner than we thought, but she came. I was 19 years old and a junior in college. We didn't plan to have a family so soon, but it happened and it was a blessing. Deanna and I had been dating since 9th grade. We didn't have any money, but I think we handled it well. I tried to maintain my grades at school, maintain my level of play in football and tried to be as good a dad as I could. I look back and I'm kind of surprised I did it all as well as I did. What helped out was having a great daughter.

Deanna's a great athlete in her own right. Our daughter, Brittany, is also very competitive. So we're all very much alike.

I NEVER THOUGHT BEING A FATHER AND SPENDING TIME AT HOME WITH WIFE AND FAMILY WOULD BE SO REWARDING. BUT I REALLY LOVE THE TIME WE HAVE TOGETHER.

MY DAUGHTER **BRITTANY** IS DIFFERENT THAN I WAS AT HER AGE.

She's more into artwork and computers, things like that. You couldn't keep me in the house growing up. Of course, I had two brothers to keep me occupied. But there was nothing else to do back then. We didn't have cable television or video games so it wasn't any fun staying inside. But she has been able to see things most people never get a chance to see in their lives. She has been on the Jay Leno Show, she has been on Good Morning America, she has traveled to New York City and California, she has been on private planes and has traveled to professional football games. With all that, she has handled it very well. I think she looks at Deanna and me and knows we aren't any different than anyone else. We come home and we get our feet dirty just like everyone else. She likes to go back home just like we do.

MY WIFE GOT ME A LITTLE YORKSHIRE TERRIER FOR MY BIRTHDAY THREE OR FOUR YEARS AGO AND I NEVER THOUGHT I WOULD LIKE THAT DOG. WHEN I GREW UP WE

ALWAYS HAD BIG DOGS, LABRADORS, ST. BERNARD'S. THIS WAS A LITTLE HOUSE DOG THAT WEIGHED ABOUT A POUND. BUT I LOVE THAT DOG. IT'S PART OF THE FAMILY NOW.

JAZZY'S FULL GROWN NOW

0:89

AND SHE'S UP TO A POUND AND A HALF.

THE SPECIAL OLYMPICS
ALWAYS HAVE BEEN IMPORTANT TO ME.

My mother was a special education teacher when I was growing up. I remember going to her classes and spending time with these special kids. My mother was so great with them. She always tried to bend the rules a little and give them experiences they might not otherwise have had a chance to enjoy. The thing I remember most is that no matter how bad my day was, they made me feel like their day was always perfect. It seemed like they always were smiling. I used to think they just didn't know how unfortunate they were. Maybe we're the ones that don't know how fortunate they are.

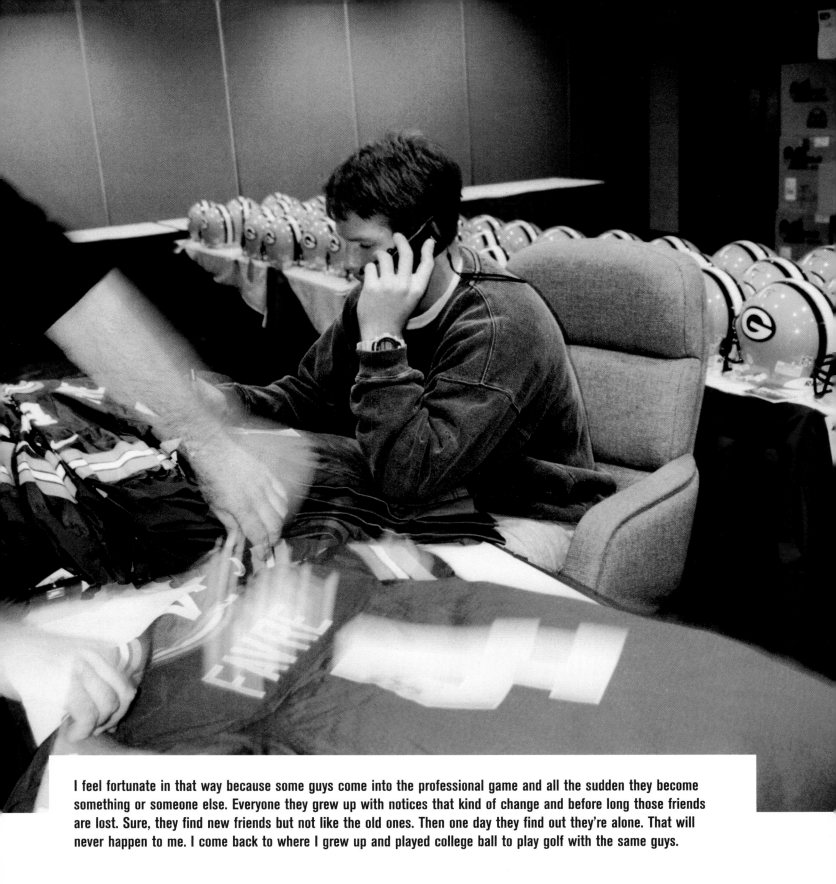

I feel fortunate in that way because some guys come into the professional game and all the sudden they become something or someone else. Everyone they grew up with notices that kind of change and before long those friends are lost. Sure, they find new friends but not like the old ones. Then one day they find out they're alone. That will never happen to me. I come back to where I grew up and played college ball to play golf with the same guys.

The most successful and also the most liked people are the ones who act like they have nothing and, as a result, have it all. I don't see why that's unique, but it does seem to be. I see guys who have not set foot on the field but walk around like they are suddenly the coolest people in the world. That's not them. I could act that way with what I've accomplished. But that's not me either. I've had people approach me in the grocery store and say, 'What are you doing here? Don't you have someone to do that for you?' People think that way. I would never ask someone a question like that. Why shouldn't I be a normal

0:92

person? Why shouldn't I walk around in shorts and flip flops instead of a suit and tie? Some people have an idea of who and what I should be given what I've accomplished on the football field. But I don't see why one should have anything to do with the other. That guy throwing touchdown passes is the same guy wearing the shorts. When I blew out the right front tire on my pick-up truck on Super Bowl Sunday, my brother-in-law and I went to change it at halftime. Once the tire was on I forgot all about it. It drove my friends crazy because I was driving around with this little tire on the front for three or four months. Didn't bother me at all.

I could be just about any way I wanted and no one probably would think much of it. But I want to be the person I was in high school and junior high school. Fortunately, I have enough money to pay bills and I can buy things if I want. But I've stayed away from buying a bunch of cars or a fleet of boats. That's not me. We have nice things, my daughter has nice things. If we go out to dinner with friends or family, we'll treat. If I go golfing with some of my

friends back home, then I'll pay for golfing. To me, that's what having money is all about. If we need something, then we don't have to worry about being able to get what we need. But you can help people out. If money doesn't do those things, then what's the point?

I ENJOY HUNTING AND

0:96

FISHING.

I'm not one of those guys who won't have something to do when I retire from professional football. I like to golf and I really don't get to hunt or fish as much as I'd like because the peak season for both of them is during the football season.

0:97

"I THINK HE WENT OUT ONE MORNING, ALL BUNDLED UP BECAUSE IT WAS KIND OF COLD,

AND HE WAS GOING DEER HUNTING.

0:98

ON THE OTHER SIDE OF THE CREEK, I GUESS HE CAME RIGHT UP ON A DEER, AND IT SCARED BOTH OF THEM TO DEATH. YOU KNOW, ONE OF THOSE THINGS WHERE BRETT RAN ONE WAY AND THE DEER RAN THE OTHER WAY. THAT'S WHEN I KNEW HE PROBABLY WASN'T REALLY GOING TO BE MUCH INTO HUNTING."

BONITA FAVRE, BRETT'S MOTHER.

I've always been very comfortable in public speaking situations. My father was a football coach so i grew up going to banquets

"JUST HAVE FUN. IF YOU HAVE

and watching him speak. He always made it look so easy. I asked him how he did it and he said,

FUN THEN EVERYONE ELSE WILL HAVE FUN."

I don't know how long I'll play, but I'd like to think my career still has another five to 10 years.

If my body holds up I think the best years are yet to come. Generally, I don't plan that far in advance but I have thought about what I'll do when I finish playing. I know leaving the game will be difficult for me. At the same time, I'm looking forward to that time. From as far back as I can remember,

football has been my life. Hopefully Deanna and I will have more kids and I'll have the opportunity and time to watch them grow up. Somebody asked me once if I'd ever go into politics

after I've finished playing. I don't think so. You can't believe in everything and please everybody all the time. I'm the kind of guy who would want to make everybody happy and obviously that's not possible. So getting away from the professional football life probably will be the best thing. We hope to have

some property with horses, cows and a pond or two. That sounds like home to me.

I've been all over the country to just about every major city in the United States. I've seen a lot more than I ever would have thought coming from southern Mississippi. But that's where I'll go when I'm through playing. We bought 450 acres an hour from where I grew up and we're going to build a house. My daughter loves it down there and my

wife and I do too. That's an easy decision for me. It's always been easy to go back home in the offseason. I never had any desire to stay in some big city or move to Florida or someplace like that. I don't know why people would want to do that.

HOME ALWAYS WILL BE
HANCOCK COUNTY

AND THAT'S WHERE I'LL GO ONCE I'M FINISHED PLAYING.

1:06

I love Green Bay, the people, the atmosphere, everything about the place. I can't imagine playing for another team in another city. But I do appreciate going back home in the off-season. When the time comes, I'll go right back home and hang out with all the same people I hung out with growing up. Some people just come from a place. But I feel like I am that place.

I'VE LEARNED TO TAKE THE GAME AND MY CAREER MOMENT TO MOMENT. RIGHT NOW, I ENJOY PLAYING FOOTBALL. I STILL LOOK FORWARD TO EVERY PRACTICE AND EVERY GAME.